What is Montserrat?

Publicacions de l'Abadia de Montserrat

Text: Maur M. Boix
Translation: Kenneth Lyons
Text review: Robert Jones
Layout: Marc Ancochea

First edition: April 1998
Third edition: November 2014
© Publicacions de l'Abadia de Montserrat – www.pamsa.cat
ISBN: 978-84-9883-709-4
Dep. leg.: B. 21.230-2014
Printed at Tallers Gràfics Soler, S. A. – c. Enric Morera, 15 – 08950 Esplugues de Llobregat

Contents

Montserrat is a mountain that astonishes you the moment you see it, for it is so different from all others. Seen from the distance, looming up alone out of the landscape, it is bound to attract your attention. Depending on where you see it from, its silhouette is reminiscent of the toothed blade of a saw. And here you have the clue to its name, for the Catalan word *Montserrat* means "sawn mountain". But you will find this name even more felicitous as you approach the mountain and start climbing. The shape of the

The unmistakable bulk of Montserrat rises almost vertically from the surrounding lowlands.

rocks might make you imagine that Montserrat had been carved, wrought or sawn by some prodigious hand. In fact the poet Verdaguer, one of the great epic writers in our literary history, envisaged the mountain as something sawn by the angels.

At all events, whether by angelic hands or natural forces, the saw above a design of stylized crags is the heraldic symbol of Montserrat.

The mountain is situated almost at the very centre of Catalonia, about thirty kilometres north-west of Barcelona. It is 10 kilometres in length by 5 in width, at its widest point, with an undulating perimeter of about 25 kilometres. Rising almost perpendicularly out of the surrounding lowlands, it reaches a height of 1,235 metres at its highest point, which is called the peak of St. Jerome. Geologically, the sedimentary origin of the massif is quite evident. The rocks in it are formed of a conglomerate of pebbles, principally limestone, but with fragments of quartz, slate and porphyry, all bound together by a natural cement.

This produces an extremely characteristic stone, with colourings that have a very striking effect when it is polished. The atmospheric agents —the wind, rain and snow, the heat, cold and mist— have worked upon the rocky blocks for many thousands of years to mould them into the weird shapes that so surprise us and stimulate our imagination today. While poets have compared the mountain to a great castle, a ship or a gigantic organ, or have presented it as an immense conflagration of petrified flames, there are many particular peaks or crags which have been given popular names of their own because of some fancied resemblance to human figures, animals or objects: *the spellbound giant, the friar, the sentinel, the doll, death's-head, the finger, the camel, the elephant's trunk, the cat's head, the parrot, the hood, the bell, the little chair, the dice.*

Just as surprising as the rocks themselves, however, with all their capricious shapes, is the vegetation you find in Montserrat in such variety and abundance, despite the lack of soil and the scarcity of water. Here, indeed, we can find over half of the three thousand species of plants classified in the whole of Catalonia. Besides, the trees and bushes of the mountain, in their contrasts with the fantastic figurations of the rocks (contrasts sometimes heightened even further by the swirling mist), form perspectives and hidden corners of singular beauty.

There is also a small but very interesting selection of fauna, with a variety of birds and insects. Apart from the better known and most frequented areas around the sanctuary itself, the mountain offers many attractions to hikers and tourists. Its principal interest, however, is for climbers. Side by side with "steeples" of up to 30 metres they will find sheer bluffs of nearly 400; indeed, the special techniques needed for their ascent permit us to speak quite properly of a Montserrat school of climbing.

Visible from a vast area of Catalonia, like an unmistakable sign in the centre of the horizon, over the centuries the mountain has quite naturally become a patriotic symbol. We frequently find allusions to Montserrat in the escutcheons and emblems of private persons and widely differing organizations.

It should be pointed out, finally, that the mountain of Montserrat, particularly thanks to Germanic romanticism, has received the aura of a symbol of spiritual elevation, of inner uplift. After reading Wilhelm Humboldt's account of his visit to the monastery, Schiller said that "Montserrat sucks a man in from the outer to the inner world". And Goethe, towards the end of his life, wrote: "Nowhere but in his own Montserrat will a man find happiness and peace". It is not absolutely certain, however, that Wagner took his inspiration from Montserrat in writing *Parsifal*.

At first sight it may seem difficult to climb to the top of Montserrat. Nevertheless, visitors to the mountain, who have always been numerous in proportion to their time, have always been able to count on whatever means of transport existed in that period. After the bridle paths, which had succeeded the original woodland tracks, came stagecoaches, followed first by a rack rail train and then by aerial cable cars, all of which contrast with the swarming buses of today.

As early as the twelfth century the abundance of visitors is mentioned in an illuminated manuscript. Today, what with pilgrims and

The natural beauty of the mountain amidst the grandeur of the surrounding crags makes it a favourite goal for tourists, local visitors and, most particularly, climbers.

tourists, Montserrat is more crowded every day. The exact statistics in this respect, of course, are not easy to determine. But when we attempt to evaluate them we should not forget a circumstance that may give us an ultimate idea of the mountain's importance: Montserrat is not on the road to anywhere else. This means that it requires a special journey. Quite simply, therefore, it is a mountain which you climb for its own sake —and then come down and, with a possibly unforgettable impression, resume your everyday life.

Montserrat has become a literary symbol of the inner of view the elevation of the spirit.

The mountain of Montserrat must have taken on a religious significance at a very early date. Even if we ignore the invented legend according to which a temple dedicated to Venus had been built there in pagan times and was destroyed by the miraculous intervention of the Archangel Michael, a figure connected with many other mountains, there are indications of the presence of hermits on the mountain as early as the eighth century. The first trustworthy reference, however, dates from the latter part of the ninth century, just after the reconquest of this area from the Moors. Shortly after that there is documentary evidence of the names of four hermitages, one of which — dedicated to the Blessed Virgin under the name of St. Mary— was the origin of the present sanctuary.

The hermitage of St. Iscle (Acisclus), which still exists today, gives us a fair idea of those earliest beginnings.

In the first third of the eleventh century the abbot-bishop Oliba, a figure of the utmost importance in the formation of medieval Christendom in Catalonia, founded a little monastery beside the hermitage of St. Mary. This foundation grew rapidly, thanks to the fame of the miracles wrought there by the Blessed Virgin. The presence of St. Mary on Montserrat was given material expression, between the twelfth and thirteenth centuries, in the image which still presides over the monastery. Venerated down through the ages, it is held in high esteem both as a religious treasure and for its artistic value. It is a Romanesque sculpture, later retouched, with delicately stylized features. The dark colour of the face, by reason of which it is classified among the black Virgins, has given rise to the familiar name of *La Moreneta* (The little dark one) by which it is known to the devout in Catalonia.

The monks settle permanently in the monastery to carry on their twin activities of prayer and work.

The fame of Montserrat very soon spread beyond the surrounding area. Pilgrims to Santiago de Compostela made it known along their way, while King Alfonso X of Castile (Alfonso the Wise) devoted six of his Canticles to St. Mary of Montserrat.

The devotion to this virgin spread eastwards with the Mediterranean conquests of the Catalan-Aragonese monarchy: throughout their Italian territories there were over a hundred and fifty churches or chapels dedicated to the Madonna of Montserrat. At a later period the imperial dynasty of Spain consolidated the cult of the Moreneta in central Europe —in Bohemia and above all in Austria— and carried it westwards with the discovery and conquest of America, which had links with Montserrat from the very beginning thanks to the presence at Columbus' side of a former hermit on the mountain, Bernat Boil, who thus became the first missionary of the new world. The first churches in Mexico, Chile and Peru were dedicated to the Virgin of Montserrat, while the name of Montserrat was also given to an island, to different mountains and to several towns and villages.

Today, at a time of reassessment and adaptation, Montserrat endeavours to provide for the needs of a rapidly changing world.

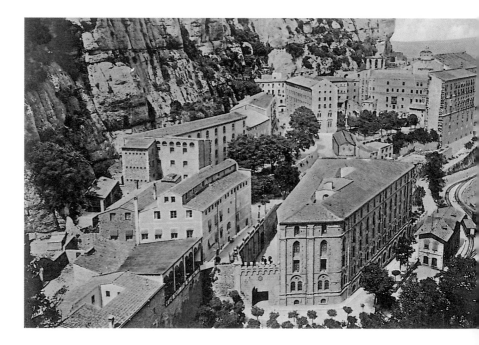

In Brazil the Portuguese missionaries founded two monasteries, still flourishing today, under the name of Montserrat.

This expansion in all directions, thanks to which the Virgin of Montserrat became the first of the names of Mary to be known on a really world-wide scale, was stimulated by the favour of popes and kings, by the presence of saints and other illustrious pilgrims, by the attention of artists and men of letters and by the ever-growing number of devotees. In our time any kind of list might sound rather boastful, but the number of historic figures connected with the sanctuary is considerable, whether they visited it personally or referred to it in their works. Pope Julius II, while still a cardinal, was a commendatory abbot of the monastery and he commissioned the building of the Gothic cloister; John XXIII stayed in Montserrat as Cardinal Roncalli; the Emperor Charles V and Philip II of Spain both died with blessed candles from the sanctuary in their hands; Louis XIV of France paid for intercessory prayers to be said at Montserrat for the queen mother; Goethe and Schiller both wrote about the moun-

tain; the house in Vienna where Beethoven died was an ancient fief of Montserrat; finally, the Emperor Ferdinand III of Austria made generous endowments to the monastery. Particularly worth mentioning is the presence at different times of saints such as St. Peter Nolasco, St. Raymond of Penyafort, St. Vincent Ferrer, St. Francis of Borja, St. Aloysius Gonzaga, St. Joseph of Calasanz, St. Anthony M. Claret and St. Joaquima of Vedruna, among others. But perhaps the most notable case is that of St. Ignatius Loyola, the knight who, di-

The basilica, which was built in the sixteenth century, is the venue for all kinds of religious events.

Idyllic view of the shrine and the monastery's kitchen garden. Engraving of Alexandre de Laborde (early nineteenth century).

rected by the monk who had confessed him, embarked upon his new life in Montserrat, after spending his knightly vigil before the image of St. Mary. Simultaneously with this expansion in the outer world, the sanctuary itself continued to grow. The original hermitage had been replaced at an early date by a Romanesque chapel, the portal of which still exists. The basic fabric of the present church was built over a period of thirty years or more during the sixteenth century; 66 metres long by 31.45 wide and 23.32 high, with walls over a metre thick; exceptional proportions, especially considering its situation. The monastery was enlarged to provide new offices and more accommodation for pilgrims. The fame of the hermitages, scattered among the crags and increasing in number until there were thirteen in all, often with foreign hermits, now reached its zenith. But it was in the very heyday of this long prosperity that the sanctuary suffered almost total destruction during the Napoleonic invasion, which was made even more complete by the civil wars and revolutionary disturbances of the time. With its building fired and sacked, Montserrat was reduced to ruins. The monks had fled, the image of the Virgin was hidden and the mountain ceased to be a place of pilgrimage.

The sanctuary has overcome the ravages of various eras in the past, and welcomes thousands of visitors and pilgrims.

The reconstruction, however, was miraculously rapid. The 19th-century reawakening of the Catalan consciousness known as the *Renaixença* (Rebirth), which began in the world of letters, centred its religious and patriotic ideals on Montserrat. The vigorous action of important ecclesiastic figures — bishops, preachers and writers, as well as the monks themselves— gave the sanctuary new vitality and prepared its spiritual and material rebuilding. Of decisive importance in this task was the succession of abbots of forceful spiritual and human personality —Muntadas, Marcet, Escarré— thanks to whom Montserrat soon reached a new plenitude. The hiatus of the Spanish Civil War (1936-1939) again left the mountain unvisited, but did not greatly affect the buildings of the sanctuary, which were saved by the autonomous government in Barcelona. When the community regained possession of the monastery, the remains of some of the twenty-three monks killed away from the mountain, at different times and places, were brought back to be buried there.

Today

Today, in an age of questioning and adaptation, Montserrat endeavours to respond to the needs of a world that is evolving very rapidly; with uncertainties and difficulties, but without ever losing those time-honoured values that are still meaningful and valid.

First of all, for Catalonia. Many of the Catalan faithful are still very conscious of the fact that the Virgin of Montserrat was declared the patron saint of the dioceses of Catalonia by Leo XIII. In the religious sense, therefore, they love the sanctuary as something peculiarly their own. Montserrat does not belong to one group or another, but to all. But it should be very particularly emphasized that this sense of belonging or adhesion is also shared, in their own way, by non-believers. In Montserrat, a rallying centre with special powers of attraction, differences are easily forgotten in the spirit of the open-minded gatherings. For many of the faithful a visit to the sanctuary at least once a year is almost an obligation, though the increasing ease of in-

The faithful take an active part in the rites of the basilica.

dividual or family travel has meant fewer collective pilgrimages from villages or parishes. The fact remains that one way or another —in organized pilgrimages, in private groups for company or organization outings, with the family or alone— Catalans come up to Montserrat very often. Each visit is like a holiday for them; the mass gatherings in the sanctuary frequently strike a characteristic note of popular recreation, one that is particularly symbolized, as everywhere else in Catalonia, by the dancing of the sardana, the Catalan round dance.

The faithful take an active part in the cult of the basilica. Many of them visit the cave where legend tells us the image of the Virgin was found, follow the mysteries of the monumental Rosary and do the Stations of the Cross. Ever more numerous are those who seek new expression of their faith in conferences and special meetings, especially for young people. The sanctuary is also visited by pilgrimages of invalids.

As for private visits to Montserrat, we might say that there is hardly any important event in the lives of the Catalan faithful —anniver-

saries, jubilees, graduations, family feast days— that does not bring them to the sanctuary. In the case of weddings, particularly, there is a saying that "a man isn't properly married till he's taken his wife to Montserrat".

In groups or individually, then, the faithful are active participants in the ceremonies of the basilica, united by prayer with the community of the monks; they take part, above all, in the solemn celebration of the Eucharist, but also in the monastery vespers followed by the

traditional Salve of Montserrat sung by the famous Escolania, or choir school. The liturgy of the monks is in Catalan, the mother tongue of the country, though with special attention —through appropriate readings and prayers— to other linguistic communities, who can always be sure of hearing celebrations in their own languages. In the basilica visitors to the mountain and most particularly tourists can attend the midday Salve Regina sung by the Escolania and preceded by an ecumenical prayer. The faithful pray before the niche of the Virgin at all hours of the day. The traditional offering of candles, now replaced by little lamps, tends to become an act of fraternal aid to charitable works. Besides the great number of votive lamps presented in recent years and hung in the church, there are always offerings of banners and emblems of all kinds of organizations: religious, cultural, social, financial, sporting, etc.

Apart from the mountain itself, there are innumerable churches and altars dedicated to the Virgin of Montserrat throughout Catalonia, and her image is venerated in countless homes. Many Catalan women bear the Christian name of Montserrat, while there are hosts of associations of every kind that have adopted this Virgin as their patron. In the sanctuary and elsewhere you can often hear the *Virolai*, that hymn of Montserrat which is one of the best-known and most deeply loved songs of the Catalan people, a hymn of praise and a prayer of hope at the same time. Catalonia, in short, is so strongly bound to Montserrat that the mountain, and everything to do with it, has become an emotive, encouraging symbol for all Catalans far from their home.

In the world at large the name of Montserrat is very widely known. Its ancient fame in Europe and the Americas has been more recently consolidated by monastic foundations in Australia and the Philippines and by the building of chapels and altars in the most diverse places: Paris, New York, Bombay, Jerusalem, Vienna, Havana, Manila, Buenos Aires, Tokyo, and Rome. The mountain receives visitors from all continents, though Europeans are naturally the most numerous, followed by Americans. Religious associations in foreign countries organize regular pilgrimages, while further testimony to the range

The shrine of Saint Acisclus in the monastery garden.

The fifteenth century Gothic cloister, partially preserved after its destruction during the Napoleonic period.

of the devotion to Montserrat may be found in the votive lamps and flags of different nations presented to the Virgin in the sanctuary. Requests for prayers to be said also reach the monastery from many parts of the world.

Though it is difficult to calculate the exact number of visitors, the annual total is certainly over two and half million. Many, undoubtedly, come to Montserrat for devotional reasons. But though there are also those who come as tourists out of simple curiosity, more than once they return as devout pilgrims. That is, in our time, the traditional miracle of Montserrat. Now as before and by ways proper to each age, ways that lead to and from Montserrat through the natural beauties of the mountain and the sanctuary, Mary brings men home to Jesus.

As a sanctuary, in short, today Montserrat is still —perhaps more than ever— a meeting place on which people from all sorts of places converge; and at the same time, reciprocally, it is a focus of irradiation of the Christian way of life, through the devotion to the Blessed Virgin, under a particular form of liturgical celebration and fraternal reunion.

On the material side, besides the basilica itself and the various offices of the monastery, the sanctuary possesses a number of buildings intended for the accommodation and service of the pilgrims. Since the earliest times prayer and welcome have been the two characteristic notes of Montserrat. What the church and the monastery are to praying, the various kinds of apartments and the different types of services are to the business of welcoming; and, though they have been renovated and enlarged several times, they always prove insufficient to cater for the ever-growing throngs of visitors.

The very size of this whole commercial complex, whether under the care of the monks or even administered through responsible laymen, may give rise to more or less open incomprehension and scandal on the part of the faithful who everywhere —especially since Vatican II— seek and demand the evidence of a poor Church. The monastic community, however, does not wish to feel itself to be the owner of goods which properly belong to their users. The monks consider themselves very strictly as mere representatives or delegates and endeavour to perform the functions of executives and administrators, especially in consideration of the religious ends to which the sanctuary is irrevocably committed.

The operating conditions of this complex, moreover, are extremely unusual from the business and organization point of view. In contrast with the winter months, when the visits of the faithful to Montserrat are rarer and shorter, the accommodation is completely taken up during the summer season (April to September). There is a noticeably village-like air about the place during Holy Week, an air that is particularly evident at the liturgical celebrations. Christmas Eve, with its Midnight Mass, is also characteristic in this sense. But during the time of the greatest crowds, throughout the tourist season, there is also a very marked contrast between Sundays or feast days, which may bring anything from five to ten thousand people to the sanctuary, and ordinary weekdays, when the mountain is very sparsely visited —and especially if the weather is bad. With such great fluctuation material necessities are unforeseeable, but everything must always be ready, with the consequent risk of losses. The immediate services of the visitors are entrusted to a staff that varies considerably on account of the seasonal workers employed, but a certain nucleus of permanent staff is always maintained. All of these staff members or servants of the sanctuary live with their families in the neighbouring villages.

Highly varied manifestations of piety are a feature of life in the sanctuary.

The recent refurbishment of the shrine's upper plaza and the new organ in the basilica are evidence of Montserrat's continued vitality.

The Escolania

When we consider the different institutions of the sanctuary, we must pay special attention to what has always been its most charmingly ingenuous feature: the *Escolania*. This is the name given to the institution, both religious and musical, formed by the little choristers of Montserrat particularly devoted to the cult of the Blessed Virgin; there is documentary evidence of its existence as

The choir school has always been a charming and ingenuous feature of Montserrat.

early as the thirteenth century. Probably beginning as a small monastic school for the children who served as altar boys, the group eventually became a music school. Indeed, considering its continued existence over so many years, the Escolania today can claim to be the oldest conservatoire in Europe. Under the guidance of monks, themselves usually former choir scholars, the group's musical training was gradually extended to include the study of theory and instruments. And so down through the centuries the Escolania has provided churches in Spain and abroad with a numerous contingent of choir masters, organists and instrumentalists and has given their early training to some notable performers and composers. Of particular renown, apart from such figures as Father Soler or the guitarist Sors, were some of the choir masters of the *Escolania*, among whom the most representative are Fathers Cererols and Casanovas.

Today the choir scholars, who number fifty-five (more than ever before), are given a musical education in accordance with

this tradition. Apart from voice training, tonic sol-fa and singing theory, each scholar studies at least one instrument — the piano, organ, violin, cello, flute and oboe — and the more gifted ones have lessons in composition. The Escolania, moreover, is a secondary school recognized by official legislation, in which the choir scholars study all the normal subjects for children of their age —from nine to fourteen.

Above all, however, the main feature of the Escolania is its participation in the liturgy of the basilica, which is the chief end of parents' sacrifice when they leave their boys in the sanctuary in the service of the Virgin. Many families still think this a great honour. Once he is admitted, after the highly competitive initial examination, the child becomes a boarder in the *Escolania*, though permitted to leave from time to time to be with his family, with whom he spends the Christmas holidays and the entire month of July during the summer holidays. There is always the possibility that after finishing his studies a boy may feel the call to monastic life and ask to devote his whole life to Montserrat. In practice, however, this is infrequent; the Escolania is not a school for vocations. Within this general framework the choir scholars play an important role in the liturgy: on Sundays and major feasts you will see them at the Mass and Vespers of the monastic community, where they sing either alone or with a choir of monks. But the most typical occasion and the one most assiduously attended, especially by tourists, is the midday Salve followed by the *Virolai*. After Vespers the scholars, alternating with the monks, sing the Montserrat Salve again and follow it with a polyphonic motet. The choir scholars' performances are particularly remarkable for their characteristic timbre, thanks to a peculiar kind of intonation which makes this choir unmistakable. The faithful who have heard these performances live in the basilica can find them again in the many recordings made by the *Escolania* and the Chapel of the monastery. Until comparatively recently the choir scholars never sang outside Montserrat. The first exception to this rule came in Rome in 1950, when a large group from the Escolania performed the Gregorian Alleluia at the Mass said by Pius XII when the dogma of the Assumption of the Blessed Virgin was proclaimed. Today, in addition to making occasional concert trips abroad, the scholars leave the mountain to participate in special religious services and civic events, as well as for invited concerts in churches and small towns around Catalonia.

The Escolanía choirboys, photographed in front of the shrine of Saint Acisclus.

The Escolanía boys' choir studies, sings and has fun at Montserrat.

A mission of service

The sanctuary of Montserrat, in short, this meeting place and centre of irradiation where the presence of the Blessed Virgin leading men to Jesus becomes particularly appreciable for the faithful, today continues in a way very much its own its long history of service to a world more than ever in need of spiritual sustenance and heartfelt brotherhood.

The Virgin works in
and from Montserrat,
in the innermost soul
of the faithful.

ontseerrat is also a monastery, though so closely bound up
with the sanctuary that many find it difficult to separate
the two aspects. From the very beginning, indeed, the sanctuary has been the concern of the monks, who have attended there to the twin necessities of prayer and welcome. For their part the monks have always found in the sanctuary the specific environment in which to follow their monastic vocation on these rugged heights.

The monks have always found in the sanctuary the specific environment in which to follow their monastic vocation on these rugged heights.

The monastic life

A monastery is a community of Christians who have radically accepted the demands of the Gospel and have decided to live their lives accordingly, with a superabundance of faith, by in ways very different from the usual ones.

The persistent quest for God by means of an explicit dedication to prayer, with close attention to the revelation of Christ, leads them to give up any normal coexistence with their fellow men. They do not deny the good things of life but, after breaking as believers with the purely material and utilitarian view of life, they give themselves up to the adventure of generous renunciation and liberating hope under the action of the Holy Spirit, who offers them the chance to serve higher aims. And this is a service illuminated by joy, in which they

seek to attain their own fulfilment in the eyes of the Church and all men and in the secret of the Eternal Father and a more intimate contact with those who come to them. That is why they need a secluded environment, in which solitude is easier to find and the practice of fraternal charity can be more constant. This is the climate that must be sought and created within the stout walls of the monastery, where the monks settle permanently to carry on their twin activities of prayer and work.

The monastic community follows the rules stipulated by Saint Benedict in the sixth century.

Though monasticism, which exists in many religions and in other concepts of life, is not specifically Christian, it constitutes a vivid expression and firm consolidation of the faith. Led by their faith, which blossoms into the greatest possible expression of charity to all, the monks withdraw from the world but do not abandon their fellow men.

From a purely human point of view, of course, and in the eyes of a world characterized by evergrowingever-growing solidarity, this life of withdrawal may seem an unfair luxury, or even an escapism prompted by love of comfort or cowardice. The monk, however, conscious in Christ of his own even more radical belonging to the fraternity of men, feels called to a personal freedom in the more exacting struggle against his own selfishness. And so, shedding material things and himself, he trusts he will be free to serve those values which, beyond immediate efficacy and mere utility, really save and ennoble the human condition. In any community of naturally different men, united by one and the same ideal, a proper organization of their coexistence is essential. There must be some statutes or regulations. This gave rise to the formulation of certain norms, based on the Gospel but modified by practice in the Church, which have come from the original community of the Apostles, constantly taken as the ideal model. These norms are established in a Rule. The monks from Ripoll who settled on Montserrat round the hermitage of St. Mary during the 11th century followed the Benedictine Rule.

Benedictine monasticism

In the sixth-century St. Benedict, the institution of monasticism, long-established though it was among the Christians, finally found the man God had ordained to channel the evangelical aspirations of the monks in the western world. His influence made itself felt outside monasticism itself, in all later religious orders, even the most recent. Through countless monasteries the open and very human spirit of the Benedictines has through the centuries played an extremely important role in the formation of the new world that arose after the final collapse of Greco-Roman civilization. That is why St. Benedict is sometimes called the Father of Europe. Briefly, the Benedictine concept is based on the idea that the objective of human life is God. The monk, then, may be seen as a Christian who seeks God fully and endeavours to recognize His presence in all things: that is why he withdraws, observes silence, reflects, contemplates, prays. Another fundamental factor is sin: the fault of man, who thus draws away from God, it is always an act of disobedience. The monk's aim, accordingly, is to return to God through obedience. This, which is a natural condition in a child, becomes a voluntary act in a man and in the Christian and the monk may reach the highest levels of love and freedom. Since, however, it is the driving force of a whole life, it must be combined in submission and suffering for reasons of love with the perfect obedience of Christ. Hence the Benedictine Rule, based on a concept which is not simply disciplinary but the foundation of a whole mystic development, is totally centred on the figure of Christ. According to this radical «"Christ-centredness"» of St. Benedict, Christ is the be-all and end-all of for the monk.

The monk may recognize Christ in his brethren, especially in the sick, and he may also venerate Him evangelically in the visitors. Above all, however, he must love Him in the person of the abbot. By virtue of the community's own election, the head of the monastery is Christ's representative in it and he fulfils the paternal functions of service to its unity and guidance in the faith, with special attention to each monk.

The Rule of St. Benedict is at the heart of the monastery's life.

The monks live in a brotherly community, presided over by an abbot.

In the opinion of St. Benedict, totally in accordance with the sacramental and hierarchical spirit of his age, the monk needs the abbot's total intervention in his life. And this is not for reasons of convenience, nor yet out of timidity or childishness. The monk, in fact, is guided by the conviction that through an integral submission of his faith and charity to a man who represents Christ to him he will —paradoxically, evangelically— fulfil his own most authentic personality.

According to the Benedictine Rule, the abbot has absolute authority in governing the monastery; he must never use it arbitrarily or tyrannically, however, but rather exercise it completely in the service of the monks, particularly those who naturally seem to be most in need: the old, the very young, the sick, the weak, those afflicted by tribulations or those weighed down by guilt. The abbot's aim should be to serve, to love and, as St. Benedict summed up, to be more loved than feared.

The Rule itself speaks of community deliberations and hints at ways of obedience through dialogue, at the same time it insistently exhorts the abbot to act with discretion and counsel. All of this brings the traditional concept closer to a moral sensibility like that of today, ever always seeking a greater appreciation of fraternal and democratic values.

At In all events, faced with the double orientation of the community life, each monastery must constantly seek to achieve at all times the most suitable synthesis, in accordance with the capacities of the community itself and of the man chosen to preside over it.

Now the monks see quite clearly that the community and the relationships between people are not something established mechanically, once and for all, but —like life, like love, like peace— must be incessantly made and remade.

And in this lies all the force —a force that demands and aids at the same time— of the typically Benedictine feature of stability, by which the monk binds himself permanently to a specific monastery, with a clearly determined contingent of brethren. Then the continuous creation of the community can achieve a more close-knit, family character. Then abbot and monks, father and brothers in the universal fraternity under their Father in Heaven, offer one another a profound, humanly heartfelt love that is full of delicacy, sharing all they are, all they have, all they know. The assembly of all for prayer, centred on the Eucharist, finds continuity in the other gatherings of the community, from meals and work in groups to recreations. This deference shown by the monks to one another extends to the strangers who visit the monastery. According to an ancient and resoundingly evangelical tradition, St. Benedict exhorts his monks to venerate in their guests the person of Christ in the form of a pilgrim. Today more than ever before, this offering of hospitality is one of the most important services the monks can render. An atmosphere of silence, a friendly conversation, life shared with men of prayer: all of these can contribute to reflection, to finding oneself, to a deeper consciousness of one's faith.

A community of prayer

The principal exercise of the monastic life is prayer. Inasmuch as he has set out to find God, the monk aspires to become a man of prayer. Having prayer means the presence of God in one's own life and this, which constitutes an ideal at all hours of the day, whatever the material occupation of each moment, finds in community some moments of greater intensity, of express dedication.

Trusting in the promise of Christ that. He will be present wherever two or three men gather in His name to pray to God the Father, the monks assemble regularly, at fixed hours, to join in the reciting or chanting of psalms, hymns and spiritual canticles, intercalated with readings from the Bible and from ancient and modern writers.

The Benedictine Rule pays meticulous attention to these hours of prayer that we call the Divine Office. There have been and there

Liturgical celebrations are a highlight of the Benedictine "Ora et labora".

The chapter house hosts solemn meetings and the daily services of the monastic community.

will be many innovations, for evolution is in all things. But side by side with the spirit of faith there is always that very human principle of St. Benedict which says that the inner disposition must be in accord with its outer manifestation; the thought must be in harmony with the voice.

In Montserrat the union of the monastery and the sanctuary enables the monks to become a community of prayer, in which guests and pilgrims are included. That is why the liturgy of Montserrat has always tended to be one of participation, in proportion to the ideas of each age. Today, too, the eucharisticEucharistic celebration of the monks, which is the crown and centre of their daily cycle of community prayer, demands greater participation on the part of the faithful, inasmuch as it is truly the most important act in the life of the sanctuary.

Very often the service of the pilgrims demands the presence of one of the monks at other special celebrations. Similarly, the ordained monks must devote themselves particularly to a ministry as traditional in Montserrat as is that of penance, the sacrament of reconciliation, which the faithful receive individually or in organized ceremonies. It is hard to forecast the future of monasteries in a society that is evolving so rapidly and when the monks, in that spirit of renewal stimulated by Vatican II and counselled by current changes, are beginning to ask themselves questions about their own identity. In Montserrat more than in most places, at all events their identification with the sanctuary makes it very clear that what is fundamental for the monks is to aspire to constitute a real community of prayer.

A community of work

Prayer must be accompanied by work, and an expression which has become almost the motto of the Benedictines associates the two ideas: *Ora et labora*, pray and work. And this means working as the monks and the people under their influence, ever since St. Benedict, have learnt to understand the term. According to the Benedictine Rule, work has a laborious side as expiation, and an immediate utility as a remedy for idleness. Human effectiveness, however, must always be pursued too, with a view to both the personal improvement of the worker and the objective advantage of the work done. The monk must not engage in just any kind of labour, but must devote himself to work that is effective and beneficial —and therefore conscientious and done with conviction and with joy.

Joyful in proportion to their worth as good workmen, the monks can engage in the most diverse activities, as can be seen in the past and present of the monasteries, where we find no uniformity in this aspect. Within the community, of course, each individual naturally tends to do the work for which he is best fitted. By and large, however, every monastery has its own specialities, in accordance with its situation and its history. And each monk, though duly taking on his share of these, finds a new way of contributing to the community. Apart from the monastery as a community of prayer, therefore, we have the monastery as a community of work.

The first task of the monks in Montserrat is the service of the sanctuary. Today the traditional welcoming of pilgrims has become a complex business indeed.

The principal part of this activity takes place in the basilica, where there is a group of monks to organize the services and attend to requests. Many other members of the community have to take part in special ceremonies, apart from their ministry of penance: from the Masses for the public at the usual hours to celebration for groups or for family feasts such as weddings, anniversaries or first communions, whenever these do not take place during the Mass of the community. To all this we must add the pastoral duties among those residing permanently or temporarily in Montserrat, as well as the tourists. Different groups of monks participate in the organization of open forums for Christian reflection, pastoral work among the young, Bible courses and conferences dealing with sacred music.

A second centre of work in the service of the pilgrims is the hotel of the monastery, where the monks direct spiritual exercises, retreats and conferences, and where they also attend to the visitors through individual contacts. Yet another activity, indirectly connected with

Guests are welcomed with great interest in the monastery.

the sanctuary, is that carried on out in the *Escolania*, where a team of monks, assisted by lay teachers, are in charge of the personal training and the musical and scientific education of the choir scholars.

Within the monastery itself, apart from such jobs as administration, material maintenance and cleaning, there is the educational work of the monks who train the young men studying for the priesthood there. Some of these professors also give classes in outside faculties or teaching centres. Special care is demanded by the monas-

The library is an essential tool in the intellectual work of the monks.

tery library, which is also open to lay scholars, with its nearly three hundred thousand volumes and its special sections for manuscripts, engravings and contemporary history. Nor should we forget the management of the museums —particularly the Biblical Museum— and the art gallery, most of the works in which have been donated by private persons. And then there is the work done, individually or in groups, on the ecclesiastical sciences: theology, liturgy, history, patristics and law, as well as philosophy and literature. But the most typical work of this kind in Montserrat has for centuries been the study of the Scriptures.

The monastery also possesses its own publishing house, which produces technical and popular publications, often written by the monks them selvesthemselves. Particularly worthy of mention in this regard is the Catalan version of the Bible, as well as the publication of scientific works, reviews and other periodicals. In addition, the monastery distributes recordings of songs by the *Escolania* and the Chapel of Montserrat.

Other monks find employment in various workshops. Finally we might mention the care of the garden, an astonishing space, carved out of the rocks and a place of peace and uplift, where the monks are often assisted in their work by young visitors who enjoy this manual labour.

With all these various occupations the monks fill their day, though without forgetting that their first duty is to the Divine Office. If on the one hand they find sustenance in it for the loftiest aspirations of the spirit, there are also many occasions when its material execution makes them feel its weight.

From the economic point of view, the greater part of all this work neither is nor can be paid for. The visitors contribute indirectly. For his part, though withdrawn from the world, the monk is also well acquainted with the problem of having more than one job and with the question of overtime. Particularly now that the life of the monastery and the service of the sanctuary are faced with increasing necessities and at the same time a diminished capacity on the part of the community. For vocations are not lacking, but they are not abundant, either.

Poverty and service

While the question of work touches in itself on one of the most significant elements of monastic asceticism, it likewise affects a fundamental dimension of religious life and Christian testimony, and one that is a subject of particular concern today: the idea of poverty.

The Benedictine Rule is extremely radical in its insistence that the monks must be poor. Many centuries before any of the modern proclamations, St. Benedict denounced the concept of private property in a monastery, not as a robbery but as a vice, a wicked habit which he found detestable. The monk must have absolutely nothing of his own: not even, according to the requirements of the Rule, his own person. He can have only what he needs in the opinion of the abbot, to whom St. Benedict, in his sacramental and hierarchical concept, entrusted the task of assessing such needs. It is the head of the monastery, assisted by the bursar, who must see to it that nobody lacks whatever he may need to do his work properly. This means that the monastery, as a community, must have certain resources. The history of monasticism shows us to what extremes this idea has gone at various times and in various places. Montserrat itself lived through a period of powerful feudal overlordship which would be hard to reconcile with the modern evangelical conscience. The Benedictine Rule, in any event, with a severity more radical than that of an absolute lack of means, aims at the conception of property —like authority— as a service. The personal poverty of those who serve disinterestedly, without seeking the least personal benefit, is not thereby diminished but rather enhanced.

However utilitarian he may seem, St. Benedict's position is right at the centre of an evangelical perspective that is frankly positive. He takes as his starting- point the idea that man was created naturally for life, liberty, peace, joy, the possession of good and the enjoyment of God's gifts —and this at all times on the community level of solidarity and social brotherliness. On the other hand, privation, suffering, death and all the other negative aspects of the human condition, though inevitable and even necessary, are meant to be only transitory phenomena. Beyond all dispossession and pain, though these will not

be lacking, the Christian mystery is essentially, through Christ and with Christ, the luminous mystery of Easter. For this very reason the monk, who has renounced all personal interests, becomes capable of ranging himself freely on the side of the destitute and committing himself —according to his possibilities— to action on behalf of freedom, dignity, justice and real fraternity among all men. As a Christian, the monk knows that he must pray and work in order to vanquish evil, in order to turn sorrows into joys; but personally, in the very thick of the fight, he feels that Christ is impelling him towards the great opportunity of receiving, in utter poverty, both joys and sorrows as ways of freedom leading to the bliss of the children of God.

He renounces and commits himself at the same time: an external commitment within a personal renunciation. In Montserrat his identification with the sanctuary, the glory and servitude of the monastery, places the monk in a situation that is often difficult but always propi-tiouspropitious to the achievement of the synthesis between prayer and work, between solitary contemplation and fraternal openness: fundamental

Relaxed reading is a traditional feature of monastic life.

contrasts, though all too often insufficiently aroused, in the life of every Christian, or, indeed, of every man. In the monastery it is more specifically a question of the contrast between the emptying of the heart, which is always prone to selfishness, and the organization of means that will give it the power to render service.

Clearly this integrating synthesis must be differently pursued by the different monks, each according to his personal possibilities. In this respect a certain variety or pluralism is inevitable. Some will hear more intensely the call of solitude, which in Montserrat has produced a long history of the anchoretic life, so attractive and admired down to modern times, as lived in the hermitages scattered round the mountain. Others will feel, today more than ever before, a stronger attraction to the pastoral life of human solidarity, and of this too Montserrat has seen some very decided examples, especially of recent years. But the common responsibility to the sanctuary, in the continuous creation of a community of prayer and work devoted to its service, will indicate the margins of difference between lives which, precisely by virtue of this service to the sanctuary, cannot fail to converge.

The monastery's garden provides moments of seclusion and comfort.

The Benedictine Rule repeatedly stresses the fact that the very centre of the monk's vocation is his duty to attain eternal life. St. Benedict explicitly quotes the words of St. Paul to the effect that no eye has seen, nor can any human understanding foresee, what God has prepared for men faithful to His love. To receive it with faith and centre on it one's own existence is what is known as the prophetic or eschatological dimension of the religious life and, more particularly, of monasticism.

The monk, though in his withdrawal from normal life he endeavours to be faithful to the profound needs of the world by which the present of the monastery is surrounded, also works with a view to living in anticipation, as from now and within the faith, of the realities of the life beyond this passing existence. Whether as a community of prayer or of work, the monastery of Montserrat must be, especially in this respect, a community of testimony. In one way or another, the monks there also feel impelled and helped on their way by the visitors, as well as by those who in distant places feel a devotion to this sanctuary of the Virgin or an enduring love for the mountain.

A community of spirit

Montserrat — the mountain, sanctuary, monastery — is, through all these specific, material determinations, a community of spirit open to all horizons in its rallying-centre of fraternity and hope.

The monks' meals are part of community life and are eaten in silence, while they listen to extracts from the Bible and very varied readings.

Chronology

888   First documentary reference to Montserrat. (Donation to Ripoll of the hermitage of Santa Maria.)

971   Birth of Abbot Oliba.

c. 1025   Foundation of the monastery by Oliba, Abbot of Ripoll and Bishop of Vic.

12th century   The Image.

1221   *Canticles* of Alfonso X (Alfonso the Wise).

1223   The Confraternity. The *Escolania* (The Montserrat Choir School). (First evidence of the presence of the choir scholars.)

1409   The monastery receives the status of an independent abbey.

1476   The Gothic cloister.

1492   The monastery is declared dependent on Valladolid. Abbot Garsias de Cisneros.

1493   Bernat Boïl accompanies Columbus. An island in the Antilles is given the name of Montserrat.

1499   Installation of a printing press at Montserrat. (Luschner)

1500   *Exercitatorio de la vida espiritual*, by Abbot Garsias de Cisneros.

1510   Death of Abbot Garsias de Cisneros.

1522   St. Ignatius at Montserrat.

1558   Death of the Emperor Charles V at Yuste.

1592   Consecration of the present church. (Begun in 1559.)

1631   Montserrat foundations in Vienna and Prague.

1680   Death of Father Cererols, Master of the Choir School.

1799   Death of Father Casanovas, Master of the Choir School.

1800   Wilhelm von Humboldt visits the monastery.

1811   Destruction by the troops of Napoleon.

1816   Publication of Goethe's *Geheimnisse*.

1821   End of the hermit life on Montserrat.

1827   Death of Beethoven (in an ancient dependency of Montserrat in Vienna)

1835   The Secularization Act: Montserrat deserted.

1844   The monks return to Montserrat. Reorganization of the *Escolania*.

1858   Appointment of Father Muntadas. Reconstruction begun.

1876   Apse of the present church, with the Shrine of the Virgin.

1880   Celebration of the Millenary. First performance of the *Virolai*, by Verdaguer and Rodoreda. Verdaguer's *Cansons de Montserrat* and *Llegenda de Montserrat*.

1881	Celebration of the Coronation of the Image and Proclamation of the Virgin of Montserrat as Patron Saint of Catalonia.
1885	Death of Abbot Muntadas (March 8th).
1895	Foundation of the Abbey of Montserrat in Manila.
1899	Verdaguer's *Montserrat*.
1912	Antoni M. Marcet is elected Abbot.
1915	First Liturgical Congress at Montserrat.
1926	Work begun on the Montserrat Bible.
1931	Celebration of the 11th Centenary. Proclamation of the 2nd Republic. Declaration of the Autonomy of Catalonia. *Història de Montserrat*, by Father Albareda.
1936	The Civil War.
1939	Return of the monks to the monastery, saved from destruction by the Autonomous Government of Catalonia.
1941	Aureli M. Escarré is elected Abbot.
1946	Death of Abbot Marcet (May 13th).
1947	Celebration of the Enthronement of the Image.
1950	The *Escolania* takes part in the Papal Mass on the occasion of the proclamation of the Dogma of the Assumption by Pius XII. Josep M. de Sagarra's *El Poema de Montserrat* (finished in 1944).
1954	Visit of Cardenal Roncalli, future Pope John XXIII. Foundation of the Abbey of Medellin (Colombia).
1961	Gabriel M. Brasó is elected Abbot.
1965	Foundation of the Abbey of Cuixà (France). Second Liturgical Congress of Montserrat.

1966	Abbot Brasó is elected President of the Congregation of Subiaco. Cassià M. Just is elected Abbot.
1968	Death of Abbot Escarré (October 21st). Completion of the new façade.
1970	Ecumenical foundation in Jerusalem.
1980	Third Liturgical Congress.
1982	Visit of Pope John Paul II.
1989	Sebastià M. Bardolet is elected Abbot.
1992	400th anniversary of the dedication of the Basilica. Interior and exterior of the building restored (completed in 1995).
1995-1996	Opening of the exterior and interior restoration, respectively, of the basílica.
1997	Opening of the restoration of *Santa Cova* (Saint Cave) (March 19th).
1997	Constitution of the "Montserrat Abbey Foundation 2025".
2000	Jubilee year of Incarnation celebration. Josep M. Soler is elected Abbot. June 10th floods and some sanctuary structures renovation.
2001	Physical study and radiological analysis of the image of the Holy Virgin of Montserrat. Renovation of the Escolania and Novitiate buildings.
2003	Opening of new rack railway (June 11th).
2004	Montserrat becames part of new dioceses of Sant Feliu de Llobregat.
2006-2007	Holy Virgin of Montserrat patronage of Catalonia 125th anniversary jubilee year celebration.
2008	Death of Abbot Just (March 12th).
2010	Blessing of the new organ in the Basilica (March 20th).
2013	Beatification of twenty-one martyred monks (October 13th).